GARBAGE DELIGHT

ANOTHER HELPING

Poems *by* Dennis Lee

Illustrations by Maryann Kovalski

KPk
Key Porter Kids

To Julian and Jake—D L

For Dillon, first teacher, then defender,
then friend—M K

Text copyright © 2002 Dennis Lee
Illustrations © 2002 Maryann Kovalski
"Alligator Song" © 2002 Dennis Lee and Phil Balsam

National Library of Canada Cataloguing in Publication
Data available upon request

THE CANADA COUNCIL | LE CONSEIL DES ARTS
FOR THE ARTS | DU CANADA
SINCE 1957 | DEPUIS 1957

ONTARIO ARTS COUNCIL
CONSEIL DES ARTS DE L'ONTARIO

The publisher gratefully acknowledges the support of the Canada Council for
the Arts and the Ontario Arts Council for its publishing program.

We acknowledge the financial support of the Government of Canada through
the Book Publishing Industry Development Program (BPIDP) for our
publishing activities.

Key Porter kids
is an imprint of
Key Porter Books Limited
70 The Esplanade
Toronto, Ontario
Canada M5E 1R2

www.keyporter.com

Design and formatting: Peter Maher

Printed and bound in China

02 03 04 05 06 5 4 3 2 1

Half Way Dressed

I sometimes sit
    When I'm half way dressed,
With my head in a sweater
    And I feel depressed.

I'm half way out
    And I'm half way in
And my head's nearly through
    But the sweater's gonna win,

'Cause the neck-hole grabs
    Like as if it's glue
And my ears don't like it,
    And my nose don't, too,

And I can't stand sweaters
    When they grab this way,
And they jump on a kid
    And decide to play.

I'm half way dressed,
    And I'm half way dead,
And I'm half way ready
    To crawl back to bed.

Being Five

I'm not exactly big,
    And I'm not exactly little,
But being Five is best of all
    Because it's in the middle.

A person likes to ride his bike
    Around the block a lot,
And being Five is big enough
    And being Four is not.

And then he likes to settle down
    And suck his thumb a bit,
And being Five is small enough,
    But when you're Six, you quit.

I've thought about it in my mind –
    Being Five, I mean –
And why I like it best of all
    Is 'cause it's In Between.

Worm

Some people think a worm is rude,
'Cause he's mostly not in a talkative mood.

And other people think he's dumb,
'Cause he likes you to call, but he doesn't come.

But I've got a worm, and his name is Worm,
And he lives in a jar with a bunch of germs,

And Worm is as smart as a worm can be;
I talk to him, and he listens to me.

I tell him the time I fell downstairs
And I teach him the names of my teddy bears

And we both sit still, and I hear the things
That you hear when a worm begins to sing –

About dirt in the yard, and tunnels, and drains,
And having a bath in the grass when it rains.

And we plan about snacks, and not washing your hands,
And the letter J. And he understands.

CARTE du JOUR

Mulligan Stew

Mulligan stew, mulligan stew,
It's quick and delicious and good for you too.
Shoot it from cannons or use it for glue –
It's mulligan, mulligan, mulligan stew.

Mulligan stew, mulligan stew,
Cheap at the price and it won't make you spew.
It sets like cement, it grows hair on a shoe –
It's mulligan, mulligan, mulligan stew.

Mulligan stew, mulligan stew,
Try it today, you'll be glad when you do.
To unplug a sink or remove a tattoo –
It's mulligan, mulligan, mulligan, mulligan,
mulligan, mulligan *STEW!*

The Summerhill Fair

I found a balloon and it went up a tree
I learned how to ride on a pony for free
And I looked at a girl and she knew it was me
    When I went to the Summerhill Fair.

The fishpond was fine, they had monsters and toads
And Dad got a plant and it broke in the road
And I think I remember which pony she rode
    When I went to the Summerhill Fair.

Next year there's a fair at the very same place
I hope I run frontwards and win in the race
And I'll recognize her by the dirt on her face
    When I go to the Summerhill Fair.

Monkey See, Monkey Do

Monkey see, monkey do, monkey went to school,
Monkey on the monkey-bars, swinging like a fool.
When he took a tumble, this is what he said,
"I didn't feel a thing, because I landed on my head."
  No he didn't feel a thing, because he landed on his head!

Monkey see, monkey do, monkey in the sky,
Monkey in a parachute, learning how to fly.
When it didn't open, this is what he said,
"I never felt a thing, because I landed on my head."
  No he never felt a thing, because he landed on his head!

I Eat Kids Yum Yum!

A child went out one day.
She only went to play.
A mighty monster came along
And sang its mighty monster song:

> I EAT KIDS YUM YUM!
> I STUFF THEM DOWN MY TUM.
> I ONLY LEAVE THE TEETH AND CLOTHES.
> (I SPECIALLY LIKE THE TOES.)

The child was not amused.
She stood there and refused.
Then with a skip and a little twirl
She sang the song of a hungry girl:

> I EAT MONSTERS' BURP!
> THEY MAKE ME SQUEAL AND SLURP.
> IT'S TIME TO CHOMP AND TAKE A CHEW.
> AND WHAT I'LL EAT IS YOU!

The monster ran like that!
It didn't stop to chat.
(The child went skipping home again
And ate her brother's model train.)

Muffin and Puffin and Murphy and Me

Muffin and Puffin and Murphy and me
Went to Vancouver to swim in the sea.
Muffin went swimming and swallowed a shark,
Puffin saw whales in Stanley Park,
Murphy got lost and went bump in the dark,
    And I had a strawberry soda.

Muffin and Puffin and Murphy and me
Came back from Vancouver, and back from the sea.
Muffin is puffing from eating the shark,
Puffin is huffing from Stanley Park,
Murphy is frightened to sleep in the dark,
    But I had a strawberry soda!

The Muddy Puddle

I am sitting
In the middle
Of a rather Muddy
Puddle,
With my bottom
Full of bubbles
And my rubbers
Full of Mud,

While my jacket
And my sweater
Go on slowly
Getting wetter
As I very
Slowly settle
To the Bottom
Of the Mud.

And I find that
What a person
With a Puddle
Round her middle
Thinks of mostly
In the muddle
Is the Muddi-
Ness of Mud.

The Big Blue Frog and the Dirty Flannel Dog

Then the big
                blue
                        frog
And the dirty flannel dog
Said, "It's time to go to sea
On the good ship *Hollow Log*."
First they sailed to Saskatoon,
Where they stole the harvest moon,
    And they hung it as a headlight on the log.

Then they hitched
                their
                        pants
And they sailed away for France,
Roaring, "Pour a pint o' grog!"
As the waves began to dance.
But the North Wind with its spray
Blew them miles & miles away,
    And it muffled up the moon in mist and fog.

As they lay
        upon
                the beach,
Panting sadly, each to each,
Magic creatures came to sing
In a wet enchanted ring;
So they lit the moon again,
And they leaped with might and main,
    And they hung it in the heavens, glittering.

Then the moon
shone
bright
All the warm and blessèd night,
Pouring glory on the shore
As they danced in pure delight,
And across the silver sea,
Flying fish came soaring free,
And they bowed three times to that majestic sight.

Then the frog
said,
"Friend,
Shall we sail on to the end?
Sail forever, straight ahead,
Far as sea and light extend?"
But the dog said, "No –
But tomorrow we will go."
So they turned around,
and paddled home to bed.

Bath Song

A biscuit, a basket, a bath in a hat,
An elephant stuck in a tub:
Seize her, and squeeze her, and see if she's fat,
And give her a rub-a-dub-dub.

A biscuit, a basket, a bath in a hat,
An elephant stuck in a spoon:
Seize her, and squeeze her, and see if she's fat,
And give her a ride to the moon.

The Moon

I see the moon
And the moon sees me
And nobody sees
As secretly

Unless there's a kid
In Kalamazoo,
Or Mexico,
Or Timbuktu,

Who looks in the sky
At the end of the day,
And she thinks of me
In a friendly way –

'Cause we both lie still
And we watch the moon;
And we haven't met yet,
But we might do, soon.

"What Will You Be?"

They never stop asking me,
"What will you be? –
A doctor? a wrestler?
A diver at sea?"

They never stop bugging me:
"What will you *be?*"
As if they expect me to
Stop being me.

When I grow up I'm going to be a Sneeze,
And sprinkle Germs on all my Enemies.

When I grow up I'm going to be a Toad,
And dump on Silly Questions in the road.

When I grow up, I'm going to be a Child.
I'll play the whole darn day and drive them Wild.

Suzy Grew a Moustache

Suzy grew a moustache,
    A moustache,
    A moustache,
Suzy grew a moustache,
    And Polly grew a beard.

Suzy looked peculiar,
    Peculiar,
    Peculiar,
Suzy looked peculiar,
    And Polly looked weird.

Suzy got the garden-shears,
    Garden-shears,
    The garden-shears,
Suzy got the garden-shears
    And Polly got a bomb.

Now Suzy's face is smooth again,
    Smooth again,
    Smooth again,
Suzy's face is smooth again,
    And Polly's face is gone.

Alligator verse, alligator verse
I found it in a book, and I went from bad to worse.
First I needed medicine, now I need a hearse,
And please take away my alligator verse!

Dinklepuss

Super-duper Dinklepuss
Went to catch the train.
Super-duper Dinklepuss
Caught it with a chain.

He hitched it to the big caboose,
The wheels began to clack –
Then super-duper Dinklepuss
Went flying down the track!

Peter Was a Pilot

Peter was a pilot,
He flew a jumbo jet,
He crashed in Lake Ontario
And got his bottom wet.

The Diner

A diner named York
Ordered rashers of pork –
    Very lean, as he wished to stay slim.
But the poor hungry pork
Grabbed the knife and the fork –
    And the diner was dinner for him.

Garbage Delight

Now, I'm not the one
To say No to a bun,
And I always can manage some jelly;
If somebody gurgles,
"Please eat my hamburgles,"
I try to make room in my belly.
I seem, if they scream,
Not to gag on ice-cream,
And with fudge I can choke down my fright;
But none is enticing
Or even worth slicing,
Compared with Garbage Delight.

With a nip and a nibble
A drip and a dribble
A dollop, a walloping bite:
If you want to see grins
All the way to my shins,
Just give me some
 GARBAGE DELIGHT!

I'm handy with candy.
I star with a bar.
And I'm known for my butterscotch burp;
I can stare in the eyes
Of a Toffee Surprise
And polish it off with one slurp.
My lick is the longest,
My chomp is the champ,
And everyone envies my bite;
But my talents were wasted
Until I had tasted
The wonders of Garbage Delight.

With a nip and a nibble
A drip and a dribble
A dollop, a walloping bite:
If you want to see grins
All the way to my shins,
Just give me some Garbage Delight –
    Right now!
Please pass me the
  Garbage Delight.

The Secret Song

I've got a secret
   Song I sing,
And it's special and secret
   As anything.

It's sort of a magical
   Whispery fizz,
Except I'm not sure
   What the tune of it is,

So I jump straight ahead
   From the shush at the start
To the hush at the very
   Ending part,

Which is actually more
   Of a whooshing and dinning –
And everyone thinks
   That it's still the beginning.

And I can't figure out
   How the words of it go,
So I leave them all out,
   And they don't even show;

And it always works,
   And nobody knows
How my magical, secret
   Sing-song goes.

Mary Jane and the Big Snow

What's the matter
   With Mary Jane?
She's stuck like a truck
   In the snow again.

Brush off her mittens,
   Wipe off her nose,
Crank up her engine
   And *there she goes!*

White on White

White on white,
    The falling snow:
The only sound,
    The only glow.

The only glow
    Is white on white.
I hope I make it
    Home tonight.

The Park

When night has come,
    And streets are dark,
The sky is like
    A living park

Where shiny creatures
    Come and go,
And shed their light
    On earth below.

A Duck in a Tub

Bubbledy-scrub,
Bubbledy-scrub,
We're washing the duck
With a rub-a-dub-dub!

A rub and a scrub
For a duck in a tub –
Oh, what could be finer
Than bubbledy-scrub?

THE TINIEST MAN IN

The tiniest man
I've ever seen
Sleeps deep in a heap
In the washing machine.

Each night when it's dark
He scuttles downstairs,
And he yawns and puts on
The pyjamas he wears.

Then, taking a bottle
From under the sink,
He fixes a mixture
That's fizzy and pink,

And checking to see
That there's no one around,
He hops in the top
With a chugalug sound.

THE WASHING MACHINE

The buttons go *click,*
The washer goes *thud,*
As he wiggles and jiggles
In strawberry suds!

Around and around
He topples and flops,
A prince in a rinse
Till the cycle stops …

The foam is a pillow;
The pillow is deep;
He dreams of ice-cream
In a strawberry sleep,

Till the morning comes up,
And the sun comes up higher –
And he pops through the top,
Straight into the drier!

And after he's dried off
The very last sud,
He roars out the door
And he rolls in the mud.

The Party

The monkey's uncle sat in a tree,
Throwing bananas at Bobby and me.
So we sent for the rat, we sent for the mouse,
And we sent for the kitty to come to the house.

The rat was asleep till a quarter to three.
The mouse had a meeting, but then he was free.
The kitty was shopping for camomile tea,
But they all came to visit with Bobby and me.

Then the cat chased the rat,
And the rat chased the mouse,
And the mousie chased the monkey's uncle
All around the house.

And when they were fighting they fought.
And when they were friends they agreed.
And when they were finished, the food was still hot,
With cake and bananas for Bobby and me.

I Put a Penny

I put in a penny in my purse
   To ease my troubled mind,
But when I went to buy some bread,
   No penny could I find.

I put a nickel in my purse
   To shop without a care,
But when I went to buy some milk,
   The nickel wasn't there.

I put a dollar in my purse
   To satisfy my soul,
But when I went to buy some juice,
   I only found a hole.

   Well I cursed the purse,
      But it could have been worse –
   I sewed up the hole,
      And I made up this verse.

Percy

Percy was a pixie,
　　A pixie of renown,
He played his little pixie pipe
　　All around the town.

He played a pixie hornpipe,
　　He played a pixie lay,
And people came from miles around
　　To hear the pixie play,

For Percy played it roundabout,
　　And Percy played it square,
And Percy played the stories
　　That were jostling in the air.

Along the streets of Kensington,
　　And in the Beaches too,
In Chinatown, and Cabbagetown,
　　He played the whole day through,

Until his pixie piping
　　Was a glory in the street,
A ticklish hallelujah
　　For the music in our feet.

And though his pipe is silent now,
　　And though the stories fade,
I still can hear the music
　　That the pixie piper played.

Alligator rhyme,
alligator rhyme,
Once you get the habit,
you won't be worth a dime.
First you'll turn to jelly,
then you'll turn to crime.
But you'll never get away from alligator rhyme!

The Big Molice Pan and the Bertie Dumb

Once a big molice pan
    Met a Bertie Dumb,
Sitting on a wide sock,
    Booing gubble chum.

"Hey," said the molice pan,
    "Gum and simmy come."
"Sot your rotten kicking pox!"
    Cried the Bertie Dumb.

Then the big molice pan
    Rank Jamaica drum.
Wide at dunce, but grows with runts.
    (Kate to strinkum. **DUMB**.)

The Bratty Brother

I dumped the bratty brother
In a shark-infested sea;
By dusk the sea was empty, and
The brat was home with me.

I mailed the bratty brother
To a jail in Moosonee;
The sobbing jailer mailed him back
The next day, C.O.D.

I wept, and hurled the bratty
Brother off the CN Tower;
He lolloped through the living room
In less than half an hour.

So now I keep my brother
In the furnace, nice and neat.
I can't wait till December
When my Dad turns on the heat.

The Operation

When you step inside the kitchen,
    Very kindly do not shout:
Poor old Hannah's getting mended
    'Cause her stuffing all came out.
There's a special dish of ice-cream
    And it's white and brown and red,
And there's cookies if we're quiet,
    'Cause we think it hurts her head.

And we never bash old Hannah
    On the floor, except today,
And my Mom has found a needle
    And she's making it okay.
And old Hannah's pretty brave, she's
    Trying not to cry or scream,
And I'm sorry that I done it,
    So I'm having more ice-cream.

When you see the operation,
    If you tiptoe you can watch,
'Cause her head is feeling better
    But she'll always have a blotch.
And be careful when you look, and
    Very kindly mind her snout:
My old Hannah's pretty sick, because
    I yanked her stuffing out.

Well, I said I'm awful sorry
    And it wasn't nice to do,
And it might have been on accident
    Except that isn't true,
So I hope that she'll be friends again
    And let me play with her,
'Cause she's special to my mind, and now
    I'm going to comb her fur.

Goofy Song

Well I'm going down the road
And I look like a toad
    And I feel like Plasticine,
And the dust between my toes
Is like a tickle in my nose,
    But the puddles make them feel real clean –
        H e y !

And the hammer with the stammer
Is a dentist in disguise,
And the flyer on the wire
    Is a wren.
And the pizza that I'll eat's a
Little skimpy on the meat, so
I shall have to lay an egg
    Or eat a hen –
        Y o !

Now I'm going down the road
And I'll turn into a toad
    And I'll play with Plasticine.
And I don't know where I'm going
But I hope it isn't snowing
'Cause my underwear is showing
And the snow will start it growing
And my buddy's sure to throw it
    On my bean –
        Y e e - h a w !

The Tale of a Tale

Once upon a time
There was a teeny, tiny tale.
It had a good beginning,
But the middle seemed pale;

And when it reached the section
Where the ending should have been,
The teeny tiny tale, alas, was
Nowhere to be se

A Walk in the Woods

We walked in the woods
Where the wild ones stay,
And they didn't show their faces,
But they didn't run away.

It was quiet in the woods,
And the wild ones heard
When we brushed against the bushes,
But they didn't say a word.

Then we waited in the woods,
And we listened to the air;
And they heard us keeping quiet,
And we felt them being there.

Baby Bird

You are my baby bird,
  Flying away.
You are my baby bird,
  Flying away.

Once you would nestle
  Each night in the nest –
High though you flew again,
  Home was still best.

Now you are caught
  In a thrill of unrest;
Daily you wonder
  If leaving is best.

Soon you will waken
  And know it is so –
One final fly-about,
  Then you must go …

You are my baby bird,
  Flying away.
You are my baby bird,
  Flying away.

The Bedtime Concert

There's a concert in the bedroom
    With the aminals and toys,
And they think they're making music
    So you mustn't call it noise.
Someone's beating on the bucket
    And he's beat it half to bits,
And it's Drumming Monk McGonigle!
    I think he's lost his wits.

And old Hannah's got the trumpet
    With the wrong end on her snout,
And every time she blows, a sort of
    Sneezy sound comes out.
But the aminals keep playing
    Like as if they never guessed
That the concert in the bedroom
    Isn't what you call the best.

And the Frog has found a whistle, and
    The whistle never stops,
So that every time it doesn't, I could
    Almost call the cops.
But the aminals keep marching,
    And they must have marched a mile,
And they're all of them so serious
    It makes me want to smile.

There's a concert in the bedroom,
　　There's a racket in my head,
And pretty soon I'll have to come
　　And tuck them into bed.
But they're all my special aminals,
　　Although my ears are sore;
I guess I'll let them play, for maybe
　　Half a minute more.

The Coming of Teddy Bears

The air is quiet
    Round my bed.
The dark is drowsy
    In my head.
The sky's forgetting
    To be red,
And soon I'll be asleep.

A half a million
    Miles away,
The silver stars
    Come out to play
And comb their hair,
    And that's OK,
And soon I'll be asleep.

And teams of fuzzy
    Teddy bears
Are stumping slowly
    Up the stairs
To rock me in
    Their rocking chairs,
And soon I'll be asleep.

The night is shining
    Round my head.
The room is snuggled
    In my bed.
Tomorrow I'll be
    Big they said,
And soon I'll be asleep.

Goofus

Sometimes my mind is crazy
 Sometimes my mind is dumb
Sometimes it sings like angel wings
 And beeps like kingdom come.

My mother calls me Mary
 My father calls me Fred
My brother calls me Stumblebum
 And kicks me out of bed.

Go tell it on a T-shirt
 Go tell a TV screen
My summy's turning tummersaults
 And I am turning green.

Don't come to me in April
 Don't come to me in Guelph
Don't come to me in anything
 Except your crummy self.

I haven't got a dollar
 I haven't got a dime
I haven't got a thing to do
 But write these goofy rhymes.

Sometimes my mind is crazy
 Sometimes my mind is dumb
Sometimes it sings like angel wings
 And beeps like kingdom come.